The Funniest Things Happen When You Look for Laughs

Books available by Dan Clark:

Forgotten Fundamentals—The Answers Are in the Box
Best or Right—Why Great Is Not Good Enough
The Art of Execution
Chicken Soup for the College Soul
Puppies for Sale and Other Inspirational Tales
Puppies for Sale (Illustrated Storybook)
Clark's Children's Classics
Soul Food, Volumes I and II (Dan's Complete Story Collection)
Privilege of the Platform—The Art and Science of Public Speaking
The Thrill of Teaching
The Book of Wisdom, Rhymes, and Wizardry
Rainbows Follow Rain
Lyrical Poetry
Only the Best on Leadership
Only the Best on Customer Service

Order at his web site: www.danclarkspeak.com

The Funniest Things Happen When You Look for Laughs

By *New York Times* Best-Selling Author

Dan Clark

CFI
Springville, Utah

ISBN 13: 978-1-59955-038-1

Published by CFI, an imprint of Cedar Fort, Inc., 2373 W. 700 S., Springville, UT, 84663
Distributed by Cedar Fort, Inc. www.cedarfort.com

Cover design by Nicole Williams
Cover design © 2007 by Lyle Mortimer
Edited and typeset by Annaliese B. Cox

Printed in the United States of America

10 9 8 7 6 5 4 3 2 1

Printed on acid-free paper

Table of Contents

Acknowledgments

For K.C., Danny, Nikola, McCall, and Alexandrea for finding wisdom, comfort, laughter, and solace in my speeches, stories, anecdotes, and words. I love you and need you in my life forever.

For my NSA inspirational, psycho, drain-bamaged, humorous, crazy friends Robert Henry, Jeannie Robertston, Grady Jim Robinson, Bob Murphy, Bubba Bechtol, Steve Rizzo, Dale Irvin, Art Berg, and everyone else in the world who has taken the time to make us laugh!

Preface

When the publishers were trying to find someone to write this book, they called up the best-looking guy they knew. He turned them down. So they called up the most intelligent guy they knew. He turned them down too. So they called up the humblest, sweetest, most sincere guy they knew. Hey, I couldn't turn them down three times in a row, so I said yes!

By profession, I am a full-time speaker. No, I did not say "motivational speaker." I don't want to be a motivational speaker. They quote shallow clichés like, "We become what we think about." That's not true. If that were true, I would have been a woman by the time I was twelve years old! I want to be an "inspirational" speaker. And yes, inspiration includes humor.

The only time we can take life more seriously is when we take ourselves less seriously. A sense of humor makes our idiosyncrasies acceptable and our short falls and failings bearable, which allows us to admit that we are okay just the way we are. For example, I was so ugly as a child that my father kept the photo that came with the wallet. When I was fourteen years old, I was so skinny I had to jump around in the shower to get wet! As a high school student, I had so many zits that when I fell asleep in math class the kids played connect-the-dots on my face!

My buddy Bubba Bechtol, president of Bubbas of America and headlining country comedian, is one of the funniest men on earth. His entire act reminds us to laugh at ourselves. He is five feet eleven inches and weighs 340 pounds. He usually walks out on stage wearing a skimpy T-shirt, exposing his navel (thinks he's Shania Twain!). His opening line is "Hey, I beat anorexia! I got it into permanent remission, and it ain't coming back!"

Another very large friend was having chest pain. I was concerned and took him to the doctor myself. He said, "I'm overweight because it's a medical problem."

The doctor replied, "The only medical problem you suffer from is that your body retains too much chocolate fudge cake!"

"But," my friend insisted, "obesity runs in my family."

With a grin and an honest sense of humor, the doctor replied, "No, no one runs in your family!"

It's amazing how much joy, pure fun, contagious excitement, and positive energy come into our lives when we find humor at home, in the workplace, in sports, during church, in school, around our communities, and while traveling throughout the world. It's true—*the funniest things happen when you look for laughs!*

It's better to
shoot for the stars
and miss

than to
aim for

a pile of manure
and hit!

Family Fun

A Twist on Philosophy

If you love something, set it free.

If it comes back, it was and always will be yours.

If it never returns, it was never yours to begin with.

If it just sits in your living room, messes up your stuff, eats your food, uses your telephone, takes your money, and never behaves as if you actually set it free in the first place . . . you most likely gave birth to it.

As a Child

We were eating one evening when my five-year-old daughter stood on her chair and reached for the bread. Attempting to teach her some etiquette, I said, "Why don't you sit down and ask your brother to pass it?"

She sweetly replied, "Okay, Daddy."

Then she yelled across the table, "Give me the bread!"

"What's the magic word?" I asked.

"Now!" she replied.

High Birth Rate

A little rural town had one of the highest birth rates in the country. This phenomenon attracted the attention of the sociologists at the state university. They wrote a grant proposal, got a huge chunk of money, moved to town, set up their computers, and began designing their questionnaires.

While the staff was busy getting ready for their big research effort, the project director went to the local drugstore for a cup of coffee. He sat down at the counter, ordered his coffee, and while he was drinking it, he told the druggist what his purpose was in town. He then asked him if he had any idea why the birth rate was so high. "Sure," said the druggist. "Every morning the six o'clock train comes through town and blows its horn for the crossing. It wakes everybody up, and, well, it's too late to go back to sleep and it's too early to get up!"

Parenting

Parents have taken communication to another level. How many times have we heard our dear mother say things like, "Don't climb up that tree. If you fall down and break both your legs, then don't come running to me!" Or, when we've been in an accident, how many times have we heard our mother's classic question, "Do you have on clean underwear?"

◉ ◉ ◉

I have observed parents spanking their sons and yelling, "Don't hit your sister!" and other parents reprimanding their daughters, "Why are you talking with your mouth full? Answer me!"

◉ ◉ ◉

When the gentleman caller pulled up in the driveway, my dad screamed, "You can't go out with him. He's driving a van."

My mother asked, "Why can't she, dear? You used to drive a van."

Remembering that van vividly, my dad responded, "That's what I mean. You cannot go out with a guy who drives a van!"

Family Relations

My friend's thirteen-year-old son said to his dad, "I'm starting to like girls, and I hate it!"

◉ ◉ ◉

A three-year-old found his dad's military identification tag and asked his mother what it was. His mother replied, "It's your father's dog tag."

The child then asked, "When was Daddy a dog?"

◉ ◉ ◉

The same three-year-old gained an interesting perspective on birth. His mother was pregnant, and so was the family dog. So the mother thought it would be a good time to explain where babies come from. The boy stood wide-eyed and watched the birth of the puppies. Months later, on the day of delivery, the same child went to the hospital to visit his mother. As he looked at the row of babies through the nursery window, he asked, "Are these all ours?"

◉ ◉ ◉

I have an older aunt who had been married four times—first to a banker, then to an entertainer, a preacher, and finally a funeral director. When asked why she had married that many times and to such a diverse mix of men, she had a great reply. "One for the money, two for the show, three to get ready, and four to go!"

Holidays

A man in Phoenix calls his son in New York and says, "I'm sorry I have to ruin your day, but I have to tell you that your mother and I are divorcing—forty-five years of misery is enough."

"Pop, what are you talking about?" the son screams.

"We can't stand the sight of each other any longer," his father screams.

"We're sick of each other, and I'm sick of talking about this, so you call your sister in Chicago and tell her." He hangs up.

Frantic, the son calls his sister, who explodes on the phone. "Like heck they're getting divorced," she shouts. "I'll take care of this."

She calls Phoenix immediately and screams at her father, "You are *not* getting divorced. Don't do a single thing until I get there. I'm calling my brother back, and we'll both be there tomorrow. Until then, don't do a thing. *Do you hear me?*" She hangs up.

Dad hangs up the phone and turns to his wife. "Okay," he says, "they're coming for Thanksgiving and paying their own airfares. Now what do we tell them for Christmas?"

Don't Worry, Be Happy

One afternoon at a sales convention, an eighty-two-year-old man stepped up to the lectern. He spoke from the heart for a few minutes and then apologized for having to leave early. He said, "I've got to go. Tonight my wife and I are celebrating our wedding anniversary. Yep. Me and my wife have enjoyed seventeen great years of marriage—seventeen out of fifty-five ain't bad!"

Family Humor

One day a little girl was talking to her mother and noticed that she had several strands of white hair on her head. She asked, "Why are a few of your hairs white, Mommy?"

Her mother replied, "Well, every time you are a bad girl and do something wrong, one of my hairs turns white."

The little girl responded, "Mommy, how come *all* of Grandma's hairs are white?"

Gender Differences

Credit Card

My wallet was stolen. I waited three months before I reported it. The police detective asked me why I had waited so long to report a stolen credit card. I said, "Because the guy who took it was spending less money than my wife!"

Blanket

A man was riding a train and eating in the dining car. The maitre d' interrupted him, "Excuse me, we don't have any more room. Do you mind if this woman joins you?"

"No," the man replies, and they share the meal together.

Suddenly the porter runs in. "There's an emergency on board. We will have to double-up the occupants."

The man asks, "You mean I have to stay with this woman? I can't. I'm a married man!"

The porter explains that it's a must. The man reluctantly conforms and walks the woman to his room. He waits outside while she goes in, gets ready for bed, and climbs up into the top bunk. He walks in, gets ready for bed, and climbs into the bottom bunk. In the dark, he hears her voice. "I'm in a negligee and it's cold. Will you please bring me a blanket?"

The man replies, "Do you want to pretend we're married, just for a minute?"

In a sultry voice she answered, "Yeah."

He said, "Good. Get your own blanket!"

Lucky Night

A guy meets a hooker in a bar. She says, "It's your lucky night. I've got a special game for you. I'll do absolutely anything you want for three hundred dollars, as long as you can say it in three words."

The guy pulls his wallet out of his pocket and one at a time, lays three $100 bills on the bar. He says, "Paint my house."

Indecent Proposal

A man and a woman meet in a cafe. The man is so taken by her that he asks, "Will you go to bed with me for a million dollars?"

"Well, yes, I guess I would," she answered.

"How about a hundred dollars?"

"What kind of a person do you think I am?"

"My dear, we have already established that. We are now merely negotiating the price."

Soup?

An old fella's buddies send him a hooker. When the hooker appears at the old fella's door, she says, "I'm here to give you super sex."

The old man says, "I'll have the soup."

Know Who You Are

Rumor had it that the rancher was getting a new bull, and his three bulls discussed it in the field. The old bull commented, "This new bull isn't getting any of my forty cows." Middle-aged bull said, "This new bull isn't getting any of my twenty cows." Teenage bull said, "He's not getting any of my ten cows." Just then a large truck rumbled into the barnyard. The back door slammed open and out strutted a humongous, snorting, ferocious bull. He stared down the three bulls and started pawing the ground. The old bull choked, "Life is too short. This new bull can have as many of my forty cows as he wants." The middle-aged bull quivered, "Yes, this new bull can have my twenty cows as he pleases." They looked at the teenage bull for his reply and saw him grunting, pawing the dirt, and staring back at the huge bull. The old bull said, "You're not going to fight that bull, are you?" The teenage bull replied, "No, I just want to make sure he knows I'm a bull!"

What Gender Is It?

- **Ziplock bags**—male, because they hold everything in, but you can always see right through them.
- **Swiss army knives**—male, because even though it appears useful for a wide variety of work, it spends most of its time just opening bottles.
- **Tire**—male, because it goes bald and often is over-inflated.
- **Subway car**—male, because it uses the same old lines to pick people up.
- **Remote control**—female. Ha! You thought I'd say male, but consider . . . It gives a man pleasure, he'd be lost without it, and while he doesn't always know the right buttons to push, he keeps trying!

Traditional Gender Differences

- **Arguments:** A woman has the last word in any argument. Anything a man says after that is the beginning of a new argument.
- **Future:** A woman worries about the future until she gets a husband. A man never worries about the future until he gets a wife.
- **Money:** A man will pay two dollars for a one-dollar item he wants. A woman will pay one dollar for a two-dollar item that she doesn't want.
- **Marriage:** A woman marries a man expecting he will change, but he doesn't. A man marries a woman expecting that she won't change and she does.
- **Nicknames:** If Emma, Suzanne, Debra, and Michelle go out for lunch, they will call each other Emma, Suzanne, Debra, and Michelle. But

if Mike, Phil, Rob, and Jack go out for a pint, they will affectionately refer to each other as Fat Boy, Godzilla, Butthead, and Useless.

- **Success:** A successful man is one who makes more money than his wife can spend. A successful woman is one who can find such a man.

Man-ness

- The floor is considered an acceptable clothing storage location for men. Why hang it up if I'm just going to wear it again?
- Just tell me what you want me to wear before I get dressed. And remember that this takes me less than ten minutes no matter what the occasion is. After all, I am getting dressed, not getting ready.
- Yelling to me across the house sounds exactly like stadium crowd background noise to me. I am not ignoring you.
- Don't ask me if I prefer one outfit over another or if a certain accessory should be worn or not. I consider this a no-win situation and would rather just wait for you to get dressed while watching TV.
- Don't ask me if I think you are overweight. If I say yes, you hate me and start yelling. If I say no, you think I'm lying and wonder what else I'm lying about. And if I say "we all are," you start crying and stop talking to me.
- No matter what, know that I love you and appreciate you for cutting me some slack and putting up with my man-ness.

If You Didn't See Me

A married man left work early one Friday afternoon. Instead of going home, however, he squandered the weekend (and his paycheck) partying with the boys. When he finally returned home on Sunday night, he ran into a barrage of epithets from his wife.

After a couple of hours of nagging and berating, his wife asked, "How would you like it if you didn't see me for a couple of days?"

"That would suit me just fine!" the man said.

Monday went by, and the man didn't see his wife. Tuesday and Wednesday went by with the same result. Come Thursday, the swelling went down a bit and he could see her a little, just out of the corner of his left eye.

When the man finally recovered, he tried to protect himself and at the same time suck up to his wife by buying her one of those mood rings. When she was in a good mood it turned green. However, when she was in a bad mood, it left a red mark on his forehead!

Housework Challenged

One day a housework-challenged husband decided to wash his sweatshirt. Seconds after he stepped into the laundry room he shouted to his wife, "What setting do I use on the washing machine?"

"It depends," she replied, "What does it say on your shirt?"

He yelled back, "The University of Oklahoma!"

A Housewife's Prayer

Dear Lord, I pray for wisdom to understand my man,
Love to forgive him, and patience for his moods
Because Lord, if I pray for strength, I will beat him to death!
Amen!

Wishing

A man and his wife, now in their sixties, were celebrating their fourtieth anniversary. On their special day, a fairy came to them and said that because they had been so good, that each of them was granted one wish.

The wife wished for a trip around the world with her husband . . . "Whoosh!"

Immediately she had airline and cruise tickets in her hands.

The man wished for a female companion thirty years younger . . . "Whoosh!"

Immediately he turned ninety!

On top of Old
Smokey
All covered
with snow

I lost
my best bird dog
By aiming too low.

Letters

The Water Closet

An English lady was looking to rent a room in Switzerland and asked the local village schoolmaster to help her. A place that suited her was finally found, and the lady returned to London for her belongings. She remembered that she had not noticed a bathroom, or as she called it, a water closet, so she wrote to the schoolmaster. He was puzzled by the initials W.C., never dreaming, of course, that she was asking about a bathroom. He finally asked the parish priest who decided that W.C. stood for Westbrook Church. This was his reply:

Dear Madam,

The W.C. is situated nine miles from the house in the center of a beautiful grove of trees. It is capable of holding 350 people at a time and is open on Tuesday, Thursday, and Sunday each week. A large number of folks attend during the summer months, so it is suggested you go early, although there is plenty of standing room. Some folks like to take their lunch and make a day of it, especially on Thursday when there is organ accompaniment.

It may be of interest to you to know that my daughter met her husband in the W.C. and was also married there.

We hope you will be there in time for our bazaar to be held very soon. The proceeds will go toward the purchase of plush seats which the folks agree are a long-felt need, as the present seats all have holes in them.

I shall close now with the desire to accommodate you in every way possible, and I will be happy to save you a seat down front or near the door, whichever you prefer.

Sincerely,
Schoolmaster

Letter from Camp

Dear Mom,

Our scoutmaster told us all to write to our parents in case you saw the flood on TV and worried. We are OK. Only one of our tents and two sleeping bags got washed away. Luckily, none of us got drowned because we were all up on the mountain looking for Chad when it happened.

Oh yes, please call Chad's mother and tell her he is OK. He can't write because of the cast. I got to ride in one of the search and rescue Jeeps. It was neat. We never would have found him in the dark it if hadn't been for the lightning. Scoutmaster Webb got mad at Chad for going on a hike alone without telling anyone. Chad said he did tell him, but it was during the fire so he probably didn't hear him. Did you know that if you put a gas can on a fire, it will blow up? The wet wood still didn't burn, but one of our tents did, also some of our clothes. John is going to look weird until his hair grows back. We will be home on Saturday if Scoutmaster Webb gets the car fixed. It wasn't his fault about the wreck. The brakes worked OK when we left. Scoutmaster Webb said that with a car that old you have to expect something to break down; that's probably why he can't get insurance on it. We think it's a neat car. He doesn't care if we get it dirty, and if it's hot, sometimes he lets us ride on the tailgate, and it gets pretty hot with ten people in a car. He let us take turns riding in the trailer until the highway patrolman stopped and talked to us. Scoutmaster Webb is a neat guy. Don't worry, he is a good driver. In fact, he is teaching Terry how to drive. But he only lets him drive on the mountain roads where there isn't any traffic. All we ever see up there are logging trucks.

This morning all of the guys were diving off the rocks and swimming out in the lake. Scoutmaster Webb wouldn't let me because I can't swim and Chad was afraid he would sink because of his cast, so he let us take the canoe across the lake. It was great. You can still see some of the trees under the water from the flood. Scoutmaster Webb isn't crabby like some scoutmasters. He didn't even get mad about the life jackets. He has to spend a lot of time working on the car so we are trying not to cause him any trouble.

Guess what? We have all passed our first-aid merit badges. When Dave dove in the lake and cut his arm, we got to see how a tourniquet works. Also Wade and I threw up. Scoutmaster Webb said it probably was just food poisoning from the leftover chicken. He said they got sick that way with the food they ate in prison. I'm so glad he got out and became our scoutmaster.

He said he sure figured out how to get things done better while he was doing his time. I have to go now. We are going into town to mail our letters and buy bullets.

Don't worry about anything. We are fine.

Love,

Cole

Freshman's First Letter Home

Dear Mom,

I'm sorry it's taken me so long to write. I've never been to the city before. It's my first time away from you, and I'm trying to figure everything out. I don't live where I did when you dropped me off. I read in the paper where most accidents happen within twenty miles of where you live, so I moved.

This place has what I thought was a washing machine. The first day I put four shirts in it, I pulled the chain and haven't seen them since. I finally found the real machine and bought laundry detergent. It said "ALL," so I dumped the whole box in. I now owe three thousand dollars for flood damage, but they deducted three hundred dollars because the carpets on all three floors of the dorms are clean!

It only rained twice this week—three days the first time and four days the second time.

The president of my fraternity fell in a whiskey vat at our last party. Some students tried to pull him out, but he fought them off gallantly and drowned. We cremated him but couldn't get the flame to go out. He burned for five days.

Three of my other friends went off a bridge in a pick-up. One was driving. The other two were in the back. The driver got out. He rolled down the window and swam to safety. The other two drowned because they couldn't get the tailgate down.

Sincerely,

Your Loving Son

P.S. I was going to send you the expense receipts you requested, but I already had this letter sealed.

Family Ties

Dear Abby,

I have three brothers. One is a lawyer, one is a motivational speaker, and the other one was sent to the electric chair. I have two sisters. One is a well-known prostitute and the other is a Communist working to overthrow the government. My mom is in an insane asylum, and the five men claiming to be my father are all drug dealers. I just met a wonderful man who will soon be released from prison for the double ax murders of his parents. We are very much in love and plan to marry. My problem—do you think he will still marry me if I tell him about my brother who is a motivational speaker?

Senior Moments

You Know You're Getting Old If . . .

- You and your teeth don't sleep together.
- You bend over to pull up your socks and think, "What else can I accomplish while I'm way down here?"
- During breakfast you hear snap, crackle, pop, but you're not eating cereal.
- Your back goes out but you stay home.
- Your idea of weight lifting is standing up, and it takes two tries to get up from the couch.
- Most of the names in your address book start with Dr.
- You sit in a rocking chair and can't get it going.
- It takes twice as long to look half as good.
- You confuse having a clear conscience with a bad memory.
- You finally get your head together and your body starts falling apart.

As a Child

Two old friends were long time neighbors living way out in the country. One day they decided to hitch up the horse and buggy and ride into town to see if they could find a little action. When they arrived there was nothing going on, so they walked the aisles of the grocery store. One old boy said, "Looky here. This box says Exlax—Makes You Feel Younger. Want to try it?" The other agreed, and they bought two boxes. They boarded their buggy and headed back home.

One said, "Let's try it," so they split a box.

Fifteen minutes later, still riding on the bumpy, rutted road, the other asked, "Feelin' any younger yet?"

"No," he replied. So they split the other box.

Fifteen minutes later, still bouncing and vibrating up and down as the buggy took them home, one asked, "Are you feelin' any younger yet?"

The other, with a pale, sheepish grin slowly answered, "No, but I think I just did a mighty childish thing!"

Things People Say

A police officer pulled over an older couple and said, "Sir, you were speeding, and you are not wearing your seat belt."

The elderly man scoffed and replied, "No, I wasn't speeding. Prove it. And I just took the belt off to talk to you!"

Exasperated, the officer turned to the wife. "Ma'am, your husband was speeding, wasn't he, and he probably hasn't had his seat belt on all day."

"Officer," she replied. "After forty years of marriage, I've learned never to argue with my husband when he's been drinking."

Talking Frog

An older man was walking in the woods when a frog jumped out of the grass and said, "Please, fine sir, if you will take me home and kiss me I will turn into a beautiful princess and stay with you forever." The old man picked up the frog, put it in his pocket, and headed for home.

On his way he stopped at the local store to show everyone his frog. Again the frog repeated, "If you kiss me I will turn into a beautiful princess."

The people couldn't believe it. "Quick—kiss it. Get your princess."

The old man paused, thought for a minute and slowly replied, "Nah. At my age I would rather have a talking frog!"

In a courtroom in Kentucky, a seventy-year-old man was called as a key witness for the prosecution in a murder trial. On the stand, the defense attorney tried to discount the validity of his testimony. He attacked the elderly man, "You mean to tell me that you saw the defendant shoot a man at ten at night?" The old southern gentleman politely answered, "Yes sir, I saw him do it with my own two eyes." The defense attorney yelled, "You were fifty yards away! How far can you see in the dark?" The old man replied, "I can see the moon, how far's that?"

107 Years Old

A 107-year-old man was interviewed on *The Tonight Show.* Jay Leno said, "It says here in your bio that you've been married seven times." The intense, energetic little man excitedly answered, "Yep. I loved them all but I outlived 'em all." Leno continued, "It says here that your current wife is thirty-five years old. Aren't you afraid of a heart attack?" The old man perked up, smiled, and quickly replied, "Hey, if she goes, she goes!"

Loving Our Seniors

My aunt felt like she had gotten totally out of shape, so she got her doctor's permission to join a fitness club and start exercising. She decided to take an aerobics class for seniors. She bent, twisted, gyrated, jumped up and down, and perspired for an hour. But, by the time she got her leotard on, the class was over.

◉ ◉ ◉

An elderly gentleman was complaining about getting old. "I've had two bypass surgeries, a hip replacement, and new knees. I've fought prostate cancer and diabetes. I'm half blind, I can't hear anything quieter than a jet engine, and I take forty different medications that make me dizzy, winded, and subject to blackouts. I have bouts with dementia and poor circulation, and I can hardly feel my hands and feet anymore. I can't remember if I'm eighty-five or ninety-two, and I have lost all my friends. But thank God, I still have my driver's license!"

◉ ◉ ◉

A reporter was interviewing a 104-year-old woman. "And what do you think is the best thing about being 104?" the reporter asked.

The woman simply replied, "No peer pressure."

More Senior Moments

Just before the funeral services, the undertaker came up to the very elderly widow and asked, "How old was your husband?"

"Ninety-eight," she replied. "Two years older than me."

"So, you're ninety-six," the undertaker commented. She responded, "Hardly worth going home, is it?"

⊙ ⊙ ⊙

It's scary when you start making the same noises as your coffeemaker.

⊙ ⊙ ⊙

The Senility Prayer: Grant me the senility to forget the people I never liked anyway, the good fortune to run into the ones I do, and the eyesight to tell the difference.

⊙ ⊙ ⊙

Rose Colored Glasses

My face in the mirror
Isn't wrinkled or drawn
My house isn't dirty
The cobwebs are gone
My garden looks lovely
And so does my lawn
No, I'll never ever
Put glasses back on!

More Fun

Ever Wonder . . .

- About people who spend two dollars apiece on those little bottles of Evian water? Try spelling Evian backward: Naïve!
- Why we say something is out of whack? What's a whack?
- About Cheez Whiz? I know what cheese is, but what's whiz?
- Why a wise man and a wise guy are opposites?
- Why overlook and oversee have opposite meanings?

Have You Ever . . .

Have you ever known someone who plays so much golf that he actually gathers his friends together to show them slides of work?

⊙ ⊙ ⊙

Have you ever known a man whose hair is so perfectly in place and sprayed down that it hasn't moved since 1977?

⊙ ⊙ ⊙

Have you ever known the classic man who has lost hair on the top front of his head and he is growing it in places he doesn't even need it (nose, ears)? His only hope is that the hair in his right ear will grow long enough so that he can comb it up over the top of his head and fake everybody out!

Finding More Humor

When all the freeway shootings were taking place in California, I saw a bumper sticker, "Honk if you're reloading." Everyone was suddenly gracious and polite. "No, please, you go first. No. I can't. You go in front of me. Please. No. You pull in." The person you let in flipped you the peace sign and the person you made wait behind you flipped you a half a peace sign!

⊙ ⊙ ⊙

Remember when it snowed for the first time in Malibu, California? Most had never seen snow before. The crazies were outside on their hands and knees snorting carefully arranged lines of it. They thought the snow was cocaine from God! "Woah . . . (sniff, sniff). I believe, I believe . . . (snort, sniff)."

The Cover-Up

Two ladies, who didn't know the meaning of being neighborly, had been feuding for months. One day they finally reconciled their differences and rekindled their friendship. They hugged and retired to their respective homes.

Thirty minutes later one of the women was looking out her patio window and discovered her dog with something white in its mouth. It was her neighbor's pet rabbit.

"Oh, no," she said to herself. "I've just glued our relationship back together and my dog kills her rabbit!" She quickly took the dead animal into her home, washed it, and blow-dried its fur into a beautiful fluff. She tiptoed into her neighbor's backyard and secretly placed the dead rabbit in its hutch and locked the door. She thought all was well until she heard a blood-curdling scream.

She ran outside to greet her neighbor.

"What's wrong?" she asked.

"Five days ago my rabbit died and we buried it in the garden. Now it's back in its cage!"

One Wish

Three guys stranded on a desert island find a magic lamp containing a genie, who grants them each one wish. The first guy wishes he were off the island and back home. The second guy wishes the same. The third guy says, "I'm lonely. I wish my friends were back here."

Rover

My dad's favorite joke:

I'd been trying to take out Milly Lou for a long time. Finally she said yes. She wanted to take me to her favorite restaurant. Wouldn't you know it, she loves chili. I was a bit nervous because I knew what chili did to me, but I was starving so I tanked it down and ate a lot more than I should have. At the end of the evening, Milly Lou wanted me to meet her family. We went to her house and gathered in the living room. Her dad, mom, brother, sister, me, Milly Lou, even the dog was there sitting by my feet. Let's face it. I'm only human and as the conversation progressed the chili started to get to me. So, I let a little gas out.

Milly Lou's dad said, "Rover."

I thought, *Great, he thinks it's the dog.* So I let a little more out.

Again Milly Lou's dad said, "Rover."

I thought, *Perfect, he knows it's the dog.* So I let it all out.

Just then Milly Lou's dad stands up and yells, "Rover, get over here boy before he poops on you!"

Food

I was sitting in a restaurant when the man in the booth next to me asked what the special of the day was. The waitress replied, "Cow's tongue."

"Yuck," he said. "How could anyone eat anything that had been in something's mouth? I'll have two eggs."

As I laughed, he too realized the absurdity of his comments and we took the conversation further. "Can you imagine the first guy who ate an egg?" I asked. "Two old boys out on the farm. One says to the other, 'Hey, the next thing that pops out of the south end of that chicken, I'll eat it. We'll call it an egg.'"

"And what about the guys who drank milk for the first time. Same two old boys on the farm talking, 'Hey, you yank on one of those long skinny hot dog looking things hanging down from under the back end of that cow and I'll drink whatever comes out. We'll call it milk.'"

"And can you imagine the first guy who ate cheese? The same old boys accidentally leave a gallon of milk out in the corner of their hot kitchen. Two months later they discover it. One says to the other, 'If you'll scrape that green and black mold off of that block of hard curdled milk, I'll eat it. We'll call it cheese!'"

The Buffet

I was eating at an all-you-can-eat Chinese buffet restaurant with three guys I used to play football with. Each of them still weighed about three hundred pounds. After four hours of trip after trip through the buffet line, the sweet little Asian manager came out and scolded us, "You big fat guys go now! You ee too much foo. I go bro!"

Insecurity

The other day someone came up to me after my speech and asked, "Why do you need all this attention? Are you insecure?"

Then I started thinking, *I guess I am insecure; my whole life I've wondered whether or not I was adopted.* Now, obviously there's nothing wrong with being adopted. I just think your parents should tell you when the time is right. So, after all these years of insecurity and wonder, I finally got up enough courage to ask my father if I was adopted. I walked into his room and said, "Ling Chow . . ."

Names

I never realized the importance of names until the O. J. Simpson murder trial. I just heard that the Orange Juice Manufacturers of Florida offered O. J. twelve million dollars to change his name to Snapple!

◉ ◉ ◉

The old rock-and-roll musician Frank Zappa had three children. His son's name is Dweezle. His oldest daughter's name is Moon Unit. Zappa's youngest daughter's name is Motor Head. What an idiot. Everybody knows Motor Head is a boy's name!

Cultural Fun

I checked into a hotel in San Jose, California. I said to the front desk supervisor, "Nice city, San Geosee."

He smiled and said, "No, sir, it's San Hozay." He had on a name tag that read *Jose*.

I said, "Nice to meet you Geosee."

He smiled and said, "No, no, it's Hozay."

I asked, "Hozay?"

He smiled again and said, "Yes, like Hozay Can You See."

We both laughed and he asked me, "When you come and visit us again?"

With tongue in cheek I answered, "Oh, some time between Hune and Huly!"

KGB

The phone rings at KGB headquarters.

"Hello?"

"Hello, is this the KGB?"

"Yes. What do you want?"

"I'm calling to report my neighbor, Yankel Rabinovitz, as an enemy of the state. He is hiding undeclared diamonds in his firewood."

"This will be noted."

Next day, the KGB goons come over to the Rabinovitz's house. They search the shed where the firewood is kept, break every piece of wood, find no diamonds, swear at Yankel Rabinovitz, and leave. The phone rings at Rabinovitz's house.

"Hello, Yankel. Did the KGB come?"

"Yes."

"Did they chop your firewood?"

"Yes, they did."

"Okay, now it's your turn to call. I need my vegetable patch plowed."

Political Fun

A man in a hot air balloon realized he was lost. He reduced altitude and spotted a woman below. He descended a bit more and shouted, "Excuse me, can you help me? I promised a friend I would meet him an hour ago, but I don't know where I am."

The woman replied, "You are in a hot air balloon approximately thirty feet above the ground. You are between forty and forty-one degrees north latitude and between fifty-nine and sixty degrees west longitude."

"You must be a republican," said the balloonist.

"I am," replied the woman. "How did you know?"

"Well," answered the balloonist, "everything you told me is technically correct, but I have no idea what to make of your information, and the fact is I am still lost. Frankly, you've not been much help so far."

The woman below responded. "You must be a democrat."

"I am," replied the balloonist, "but how did you know?"

"Well," said the woman, "You don't know where you are or where you are going. You have risen to where you are due to a large quantity of hot air. You made a promise, which you have no idea how to keep, and you expect me to solve your problem. The fact is—you are in exactly the same position you were in before we met, but now, somehow, it's all my fault."

Wake Up

A man was sitting at a table in the bar. Suddenly, two huge men came in the door, walked up to him, and beat the ever-living tar out of him. Leaving him unconscious and in a pool of blood on the floor, the two men strutted out of the bar. As they left, they stopped the bartender and proudly said, "When he wakes up, tell him that was Karate from Korea and Judo from Japan!"

In a few minutes the guy regained consciousness, stood up, wiped himself off, finished his drink, and left.

Later that day the two men came back to the bar. While they were drinking and laughing about the guy they beat up earlier that day, the same guy walked back into the bar. He walked straight up to their table and knocked both of them out cold. As he left he said to the bartender, "When they wake up, tell them that was a crowbar from Sears!"

Think About It

A man once counseled his son that if he wanted to live a long life, the secret was to sprinkle a little gunpowder on his cereal every morning. The son did this religiously and he lived to the age of ninety-three. When he died, he left twelve children, twenty-four grandchildren, thirty great-grand children, and a seventeen-foot hole in the wall of the crematorium!

Pure Wisdom

The Value of Humor

A Stanford University study revealed that children laugh about three hundred times a day. Adults only laugh seventeen times a day. I guess that's why children live longer than adults! The study showed that 84 percent of executives believe that people with a sense of humor do a better job than those without one. People who frequently laugh experience a lower risk of heart attack, stroke, hypertension, and depression. Children don't have these problems. They set up lemonade stands and sell drinks in the hot sun. They invent things like an electric hot dog polisher and take the hair balls the cat coughed up to school for show and tell!

There is a Fortune 100 company where the leaders meet once a month to brainstorm and discuss products and services. When they enter the boardroom they each put on a large, brightly colored Hawaiian shirt. The CEO puts on Mickey Mouse ears. Immediately they have permission to think outside the lines and let their imaginations run wild! As a result, the ideas flow more freely and the meetings have more than tripled their productivity.

The leaders live by three beliefs:

1. Diplomacy is the art of letting someone have your way.
2. If you can't be funny, be fun!
3. Establish a humor network by inviting people to relax and laugh around you. Leave a Slinky or Rubik's Cube on your desk for people to play with while talking to you.

Getty Up!

Lovely eighty-year-old Rose was asked to speak at our college football banquet. She stepped up to the podium and began to shake so badly that she dropped her speech; 3x5 cards went everywhere. In response, Rose leaned into the microphone and said, "Sorry I'm so nervous. I gave up beer for Lent, and this whiskey is killing me!"

Then Rose taught us the lesson of the ages. She said, "I've noticed how many of you college men are still wearing your old high school athletic letter jackets. Hey, I know you used to be a stud-muffin-hunk-of-burnin-love, but when your horse dies, dismount!" She continued, "Stop living in your past—get a life, dream a new dream, get a new horsey. Getty up, young men!"

Dead Horse

Dakota tribal wisdom says that when you discover you are riding a dead horse, the best strategy is to dismount. However, in business, we often try other strategies with dead horses, such as:

1. Buying a stronger whip
2. Changing company riders
3. Saying "this is the way we have always ridden this horse"
4. Appointing a committee to study the horse
5. Arranging to visit other sites to see how they ride dead horses
6. Increasing the standards to ride dead horses
7. Appointing a team to revive the dead horse
8. Creating a training session to increase our riding ability
9. Forming a quality circle to find uses for dead horses
10. Promoting the dead horse to a supervisory position

Hilarious Heroes

- "The secret of a good sermon is to have a good beginning and a good ending and having the two as close together as possible."—George Burns

- "Be careful about reading health books. You may die of a misprint."—Mark Twain
- "By all means marry: If you get a good wife, you'll become happy; if you get a bad one, you'll become a philosopher."—Socrates
- "I was married by a judge. I should have asked for a jury."—Groucho Marx
- "Money can't buy you happiness, but it does bring you a more pleasant form of misery."—Spike Milligan
- "What's the use of happiness? It can't buy you money."—Henny Youngman
- "I don't feel old. I don't feel anything until noon. Then it's time for my nap."—Bob Hope at 100 years old
- "The secret of staying young is to live honestly, eat slowly, and lie about your age."—Lucille Ball

Amazing Observations

- Never get into fights with ugly people; they have nothing to lose.
- All in all, 90 percent of success is half mental.
- I almost had a psychic girlfriend, but she left me before we met, so now I'm holding out for a ninety-year-old billionaire with a cough.
- On TV they show you how detergents take out blood stains. I think if you've got a T-shirt with blood stains all over it, maybe laundry isn't your biggest problem.
- One out of every three Americans suffers from some form of mental illness. Think of two of your best friends; if they are okay, then it must be you.
- Ever notice when you blow in a dog's face he gets mad at you, but when you take him for a ride in a car he sticks his head out the window?
- Ever notice that anyone going slower than you is an idiot, but anyone going faster is a maniac?

- Never raise your hands to your kids. It leaves your groin unprotected.
- You don't stop laughing because you grow old. You grow old because you stop laughing.

Thoughts

- I started out with nothing, and I still have most of it.
- It's hard to make a comeback when you haven't been anywhere.
- The only difference between a rut and a grave is the depth.
- These days, I spend a lot of time thinking about the hereafter. I go somewhere to get something and then wonder what I'm here after.

Strange Speaking

- Pick up your room.
- Will you please draw the drapes?
- I will warm up the car.
- We are throwing a party.
- I'll give you a buzz.
- Drop me a line.
- In the kitchen, I:

  Beat the eggs
  Cream the butter
  Shred the carrots and
  Fold the egg whites

- Keep your eye on the ball.
- Practice stealing bases.
- I need to catch a few winks.

Did You Know?

- I used to think I was indecisive, but now I'm not sure.
- No sense being pessimistic. It probably wouldn't work anyway.
- Dyslexics have more fnu.
- Clones are people two.
- A waist is a terrible thing to mind.
- Does the name Pavlov ring a bell?
- Join me and commence to begin to start the stamping out, elimination, and eradication of superfluous duplicate reoccurring redundancy.

Things We Can Learn from a Dog

- Never pass up the opportunity to go for a joyride. Allow the experience of fresh air and the wind in your face to be pure ecstasy.
- When loved ones come home, always run to greet them.
- When it's in your best interest, practice obedience.
- Let others know when they've invaded your territory.
- Take naps and stretch before rising.
- Run, romp, and play daily.
- Eat with gusto and enthusiasm.
- Be loyal.
- Never pretend to be something you're not.
- If what you want lies buried, dig until you find it.
- When someone is having a bad day, be silent, sit close by, and nuzzle them gently.
- Thrive on attention and let people touch you.

- Avoid biting when a simple growl will do.
- On hot days, drink lots of water and lie under a shady tree.
- When you're happy, dance around and wag your entire body.
- No matter how often you're scolded, don't buy into the guilt thing and pout . . . run right back and make friends.
- Delight in the simple joy of a long walk.

Religion

Heaven and Hell

Heaven is where the police are British, the chefs are Italian, the mechanics are German, the lovers are French, and everything is organized by the Swiss.

Hell is where the police are German, the chefs are British, the mechanics are French, the lovers are Swiss, and everything is organized by the Italians.

Why Worry?

There are only two things to worry about.
Either you are well or you are sick.
If you are well,
Then there is nothing to worry about.
But if you are sick,
There are two things to worry about.
Either you will get well or you will die.
If you get well,
There is nothing to worry about.
If you die,
There are only two things to worry about.
Either you will go to heaven or hell.
If you go to heaven there is nothing to worry about.

But if you go to hell,
You'll be so bloomin' busy shaking hands with friends
you won't have time to worry!

Religious Difference

A four-year-old Catholic boy was playing with a four-year-old Protestant girl in a backyard pool. When they took off their wet clothes, the little girl looked at the little boy and said, "Woah, I didn't know there was that much difference between Catholics and Protestants."

Church Bulletin Bloopers

- Don't let worry kill you. Let the church help.
- Due to the pastor's illness, Wednesday's healing service will be discontinued until further notice.
- This being Easter Sunday, we will ask Mrs. Lewis to come forward and lay an egg on the altar.
- Ladies Bible Study will be held at 10 a.m. All ladies are invited to lunch when the B.S. is done.
- Low Self-Esteem Support Group will meet Thursday. Please use back door.
- At the evening service tonight, the sermon topic will be "What is Hell?" Come early and listen to our choir practice.
- The Associate Minister unveiled the church's new tithing campaign slogan last Sunday: "I Upped My Pledge—Now Up Yours."

Pure-Hearted Worship

A mother took her three-year-old daughter to church for the first time. Suddenly the church lights dimmed as the choir walked down the aisle carrying lighted candles. All was quiet until the little girl started to sing in a loud voice, "Happy birthday to you, happy birthday to you . . . "

The Preacher

A preacher was making his rounds on a bicycle to his parishioners when he came upon a little boy trying to sell a lawn mower.

"How much do you want for the lawn mower?" asked the preacher.

"I just want enough money to go out and buy me a bicycle," said the little boy.

The preacher asked, "Will you take my bike in trade for it?"

"Mister, you've got yourself a deal."

The preacher took the mower and began to try to crank it. He pulled on the string a few times with no response. The preacher called the little boy over and said, "I can't get this mower to start."

The little boy said, "That's because you have to cuss at it to get it started."

The preacher said, "I am a minister and I cannot cuss. It has been so long since I have been saved that I do not even remember how to cuss."

The little boy looked at him happily and said, "Just keep pulling on that string. It'll come back to ya!"

I Have A Confession

A man goes into the confessional.

"Forgive me, Father, for I have sinned."

"What is your sin, my child?" the priest replies.

"I used some horrible language this week, and I feel absolutely terrible."

"When did you use this awful language?" asks the priest.

"I was golfing and hit a drive that looked like it was going to go over 250 yards, but it struck a phone line and fell straight down to the ground."

"Is that when you swore?"

"No, Father," says the man.

"After that a squirrel ran out of the bushes and grabbed my ball in his mouth and began to run away."

"Is that when you swore?" asks the priest again.

"Well, no," says the man.

"You see, as the squirrel was running, an eagle came down out of the sky, grabbed the squirrel in its talons, and began to fly away!"

"Is that when you swore?" asked the amazed priest.

"No, not yet," the man replies.

"As the eagle carried the squirrel away in its claws, it flew toward the green. As it passed over a bit of forest near the green, the squirrel dropped my ball."

"Did you swear then?" asks the now impatient priest.

"No, because as the ball fell, it struck a tree, bounced through some bushes, careened off a big rock, and rolled through a sand trap onto the green and stopped within six inches of the hole."

The priest sighs. "Now I see. You missed the damn putt, didn't you?"

The Monastery

A guy joins a monastery and takes a vow of silence. He's allowed to say two words every seven years. After the first seven years, the elders bring him in and ask for his two words. "Cold floors," he says. They nod and send him away.

Seven more years pass. They bring him back in and ask for his two words. He clears his throat and says, "Bad food." They nod and send him away.

Seven more years pass. They bring him in for his two words. "I quit," he says.

"That's not surprising," the elders say. "You've done nothing but complain since you got here."

The Priest

A priest was driving around observing conditions of the homes and yards of the members of his parish church. He came upon a situation where a member's car was parked in the driveway with two flat tires. It was leaking anti-freeze and the windshield had been broken.

The priest also noticed the lawn had not been cut for some time, and the lawn mower was sitting there in need of repairs. The priest immediately went to the door to find out more about the existing problems. The member said he had lost his job, and then all these other things just seemed to develop one after another.

The priest said to the member, "This is the council I am going to give you to follow. Pick up your Bible with the back toward the table. Then drop it on the table and it will fall open. You are to then read the first two words you see and they will give you direction."

The member agreed and the priest left.

A week later, the priest returned to see how things were going. He was amazed at what he saw. In the driveway was a new car, the lawn had been cut with the new riding mower, and all other things seemed to be in fine order. The priest went to the door and asked the member if he had followed all of his instructions.

To which he replied, "Yes Father, to the letter."

The priest then asked him, "What two words did you read when the Bible fell open?"

The member grinned and replied, "Chapter Eleven!"

Convert for $10

Two old Jewish men are strolling down the street one day when they happen to walk by a Catholic church. They see a big sign posted that reads CONVERT TO CATHOLICISM AND GET $10. One of the men stops walking and stares at the sign. His friend turns to him and says, "Murray, what's going on?"

"Abe," replies Murray, "I'm thinking of doing it."

Abe says, "Are you crazy?"

Murray thinks for a minute and says, "Abe, I'm going to do it."

With that, Murray strides purposefully into the church and comes out about twenty minutes later with his head bowed.

"So," asks Abe, "did you get the ten dollars?"

Murray looks up at him and says, "Is that all you people think about?"

The Devil

In the middle of a preacher's sermon, the back door of the church slams open, and in walks the devil. Church members climb out the windows, and the preacher slides out the side door. Only one good old boy stays seated on his bench. The devil walks right up to him and says, "Apparently, you don't know who I am."

To which the old boy replies, "Of course I do, you're Satan."

The devil says, "Apparently, you don't realize that with one word of my voice, I can cast you to outer darkness for all eternity."

The old boy says, "Yea."

The devil says, "Apparently you don't realize that with one gesture of my hand, I can have you tormented for the rest of forever!"

To which the old boy again answers, "Yea."

The devil then asks, "So why aren't you afraid of me?"

The old boy stands up, looks the devil straight in the eyes, points his finger and says, "Listen, I've been married to your sister for forty-two years, and there's not one thing you can do that would surprise me!"

Faith

Two nuns were driving down a country road when they ran out of gas. They walked to a farmhouse and a farmer gave them some gasoline, but the only container he had was an old bedpan. The nuns were happy to take whatever they were offered and returned to their car.

As they were pouring the gasoline from the bedpan into the tank of their car, a Protestant minister drove by. He stopped, rolled down his window, and said, "Excuse me, Sisters. I'm not of your religion, but I couldn't help admiring your faith!"

Confession

A man went to confess his sins. In the confessional he admitted that for years he had been stealing building supplies from the wood shop where he worked.

"What did you take?" the priest asked.

"Enough to build my house and three mountain cottages."

"This is very serious," the priest said. "I'll have to give you a stiff penance. Have you ever done a retreat?"

"No, Father, I haven't," the man replied. "But if you can get the plans, I can get the lumber!"

Moral Lesson

A mother was preparing pancakes for her sons, Kevin (five) and Ryan (three). The boys began to argue over who would get the first pancake. Their mother saw the opportunity for a moral lesson. "If Jesus were sitting here, He would say, 'Let my brother have the first pancake. I can wait.'"

Kevin turned to his younger brother and said, "Ryan, you be Jesus."

⊙ ⊙ ⊙

After the church service a little boy told the pastor, "When I grow up, I'm going to give you some money."

"Well, thank you," the pastor replied, "But why?"

"Because my daddy says you're one of the poorest preachers we've ever had."

⊙ ⊙ ⊙

A father was reading Bible stories to his young son. He read, "The man named Lot was warned to take his wife and flee out of the city, but his wife looked back and was turned to salt."

His son asked, "What happened to the flea?"

⊙ ⊙ ⊙

Another three-year-old put his shoes on by himself. His mother noticed that the left shoe was on the right foot. She said, "Son, your shoes are on the wrong feet."

He looked up at her with a raised brow and said, "Don't kid me, Mom. They're the only feet I got!"

⊙ ⊙ ⊙

On the first day of school, about mid-morning, the kindergarten teacher said, "If anyone has to go to the bathroom, hold up two fingers."

A little voice from the back of the room asked, "How will that help?"

MORMONS

There were three guys sitting behind three Mormons at a BYU versus University of Utah football game. The first one says to the others (loud enough for them to hear), "I think I want to move to New Jersey. There are only a few hundred Mormons living there."

The second guy speaks up and says, "Well, I want to move to Boston. I hear there are only one hundred Mormons living there."

The third guy speaks up and says, "I want to move to Alaska. There are only fifty Mormons living there."

One of the Mormons finally turned around, looked all three men in the eye and said, "Why don't you guys go to hell. I hear there are no Mormons there."

An Irish Prayer

May those that love us, love us;
And those that don't love us,
May God turn their hearts.
And if He doesn't turn their hearts,
May He turn their ankles
So we'll know them by their limping.

An Atheist and a Bear

An atheist was walking through the woods, admiring all that the "accident of evolution" had created. "What majestic trees! What powerful rivers! What beautiful animals!" he said to himself.

As he was walking alongside the river he heard a rustling in the bushes behind him. As he turned to look, he saw a seven-foot grizzly bear charging toward him. He ran as fast as he could up the path. He looked over his shoulder and saw that the bear was closing in on him. Frantically he tried to run even faster, but he tripped and fell to the ground. He rolled over to pick himself up and saw the bear right beside him, raising its paw to kill him. At that instant he cried out, "Heaven have mercy!"

And time stopped. The bear froze. The forest was silent. The river even stopped flowing. A bright light shone upon the man, and a voice out of the sky said, "You deny my existence all these years, teach others that I don't exist, and even credit my creation to a cosmic accident, and now you expect me to help you out of this predicament? Am I to count you as a believer?"

The atheist, ever so proud, looked into the light and said, "It would be rather hypocritical to ask to be counted as a Christian after all these years, but could you make the bear a Christian?"

"Very well," said the voice.

And the light went out, the river flowed, the sounds of the forest continued, and the bear lowered its paw. The bear then brought both paws together, bowed its head, and said, "Lord, I thank you for this food which I am about to receive."

Punishment

A man was sent to hell for his sins. As he was being processed, he passed a room where a stockbroker he knew was having an intimate conversation with a beautiful woman.

"What a drag!" the man expressed. "I have to burn for all eternity and that stockbroker gets to spend it with that gorgeous woman."

The devil jabs the man with his pitchfork and yells, "Who are you to question that woman's punishment?"

Divine Intervention

During my visit to the prestigious and highly acclaimed Baylor University, I was both excited and nervous about accepting a football scholarship to attend this private, conservative Christian institution. I thought it would be exceptionally stoic in its formality and totally unaccepting of humorous, off-the-wall behavior. At least until I was invited by the Dean of the College of Business to join him and my football host as a visitor in one of the classes. It was test day and the exam was sitting on the professor's desk, ready to be circulated and administered immediately following the opening prayer. Many classes at Baylor begin with an invocation. Ironically the student who was asked to say the prayer was my host, James Divine, a football player who didn't come across as much of a spiritual giant. I also knew he wasn't prepared for the test because he had been out with me and the boys the night before. So, how did he survive the moment and buy extra time to study and cram for another day? Divine prayed for twenty-five minutes until there was not enough class time left to adequately take the exam! When he finally finished blessing everything on campus and thanking God for every little thing he could possibly imagine, Divine suddenly stopped talking. Hushed silence filled the room for thirty seconds, which seemed like an eternity. Finally the professor blurted out, "Amen."

James opened his eyes, looked up, and replied, "Thank you, sir. I've been trying to think of that word for the last five minutes." As the cheering ovation from his classmates broke the tension, the test was reluctantly postponed until the next class period two days later, and each student became an instantaneous believer in "Divine" intervention!

Sports and Exercise

Competition Brings Out Our Best

Two men were hiking in the mountains when they came face to face with a bear. The bear was startled, the men were startled, the bear got mad, and the men got the heck out of there! They turned and began running down the mountain trail. Suddenly, one man stopped, which caused the other man to stop.

"Why are you stopping?" asked one man.

"To put on my running shoes," the other replied.

"Why? You can't outrun the bear," he countered.

"I know," his partner answered. "All I have to do is outrun you!"

Work Out

- My grandmother started walking five miles a day when she was sixty. She's ninety-seven now, and we don't know where she is.
- I joined a health club last year. Spent about four hundred bucks. Haven't lost a pound. Apparently you have to show up.
- I don't exercise at all. If God meant for us to touch our toes, he would have put them farther up our body.
- I have flabby thighs, but fortunately my stomach covers them.
- I'm in shape. Round is a shape.

- I don't think anyone should run if no one is chasing them, and no weight should ever be lifted if it doesn't have to be moved!
- Exercise cannot help you in midlife. Midlife is not an age—it's when you stand in front of the mirror naked and you see your rear end without even turning around!

The Diet

- If you eat something and no one sees you eat it, it has no calories.
- If you drink a diet soda with a candy bar, the calories in the candy bar are cancelled out by the diet soda.
- Food used for medicinal purposes *never* count, such as hot chocolate, brandy, toast, and Sara Lee cheesecake.
- If you fatten up everyone else around you, then you look thinner.
- Movie related foods do not have additional calories because they are part of the entertainment package and not part of one's personal fuel. Examples: Milk Duds, Red Hots, Tootsie Rolls, and Red Vines.
- Things licked off knives and spoons have no calories if you are in the process of preparing something.
- Anything consumed while standing has no calories. This is due to gravity and the density of the caloric mass.
- Anything consumed from someone else's plate has no calories since the calories rightfully belong to the other person and will cling to his or her plate.
- Remember, the devil is strong and tricky. If you eat something you should not, the devil made you do it. Darn that devil!

Abraham and Moses

Abraham and Moses were playing golf. They came to a par three hole. Moses stepped up to hit the ball and his caddy said, "Use a six iron."

Moses asked, "What would Arnold Palmer use?"

The caddy answered, "A nine iron."

Moses pulled out his nine iron and hit the ball right into the water. The gallery of backed-up, delayed golfers moaned as they watched him lay down his club, walk out and part the water, pick up his ball, walk back, and tee it up again. His caddy again handed him a six iron, but Moses said, "No, hand me my nine." Again he hit it into the water. He threw down his club, walked again down to the pond, and parted the water to retrieve his ball.

While he was gone, a disgruntled golfer in the foursome behind them yelled, "Hey, who does this guy think he is—God?"

The caddy turned and answered, "No, sir. He thinks he's Arnold Palmer!"

LITTLE LEAGUE UMPIRE

One summer I worked as a Little League umpire. During one game a nine-year-old rookie came up to bat against an all-star pitcher who was twelve. The pitcher took a mighty wind up, reared back, and threw a fast ball.

"Strike," I called.

The young batter said, "C'mon, ump, that wasn't a strike."

I said, "Why? Did you see it?"

He replied, "No, but it sounded high."

KEEP SWINGING

One year we had an inter-school boxing tournament to raise money for charity. I volunteered to fight a guy, so I needed a trainer/manager for my corner. I asked a favorite teacher, Coach Ted Weight, to assist me. Round one was brutal as my giant opponent proceeded to rearrange my face. After round one was finally over, I staggered back to my corner all beaten up and dejected. I sat down on the stool, looked up at Coach Weight for some encouragement, and asked, "Did I hit him at all? Am I doing any damage?"

Coach solemnly replied, "No, but keep swinging. Maybe the draft will give him a cold."

Boxing

A high school senior wanted to be the state heavyweight boxing champion. He found a trainer and wanted to start working out. However, his trainer told him he didn't need to do anything except think positive. His first fight night arrived, and he was excited. Round one began, and he was beat up. He staggered back to his corner, sat on the stool, and asked his trainer, "How am I doing?"

The trainer replied, "You're doing great. Just keep thinking positive. The guy hasn't even hit you yet."

Round two began, and he was again beat up so badly he crawled back to the stool, in his corner. Bloody and exhausted, he again asked his trainer, "How am I doing?"

The trainer replied, "You're doing great. Just keep thinking positive. The guy hasn't even hit you yet."

To this, the boxer immediately responded, "OK, but could you keep an eye on the referee, cause somebody out there is beating the crap out of me!"

Charity Golf

The first time I played in a celebrity golf tournament it took so long that my clothes had gone out of style by the time we finished eighteen holes. One guy in my foursome got the sports mixed up at the first tee. He put on his golf glove, and when a guy in the team ahead of us addressed his ball, he started yelling, "Hey batter batter, swing, batter batter!" I should have known it was going to be a long day when he lost his ball in the ball washer! It was finally his turn to hit, and he swung a mighty swing. He whiffed and completely missed the ball. He took a second swing and whiffed again. He took a third mighty swing and missed, but this time his club blew the ball off the tee! As he bent over to place his ball back onto the tee, the starter made us all laugh when he commented, "Tough course, isn't it?"

We had to wait until he hit it before we knew which course we were playing. When he did hit it, he turned golf into a contact sport. He finally got hold of a drive but hit a man right smack-dab in the shoulder. The man was so mad that he pulled off the highway and came and found him!

As we walked along the eighteenth hole, he commented to the course marshal who had been following us, "Boy oh boy, this is a rough course." The marshal winced, "Actually, sir, you haven't been on the actual course for over an hour!"

So will I participate in a charity tournament again? You bet I will. This experience was the inspiration for three of my newest books. They should easily be national best-sellers: *How to Line Up Your Fifth Putt*, *Great Second Shots Off the Ladies Tee*, and *109 Things Your Wife Wants You to Think about While You're Hitting Your Mulligan.*

Loft

Three guys are golfing with the club pro. First guy tees off and hits a dribbler about sixty yards. He turns to the pro and says, "What did I do wrong?"

The pro says, "Loft."

The next guy tees off and hits a duck hook into the woods. He asks the pro, "What did I do wrong?"

The pro says, "Loft."

The third guy tees off and hits a slice into a pond. He asks the pro, "What did I do wrong?"

The pro says, "Loft."

As they're walking to their balls, the first guy finally speaks up. He says to the pro, "The three of us hit completely different tee shots, and when we asked you what we did wrong, you answered the same exact answer each time. What is a loft?"

The pro says, "Lack Of Flippin' Talent."

Bowling

Why is bowling so popular? You put on a polyester shirt with a team name patch on the back like "Morris Meat Company" and a cursive name embroidered on the front. It doesn't even have to be your name, but to be an authentic shirt thought to be coveted by all who dream of owning their own trailer home, it must have a fancy name on the front.

Then you take a big, heavy ball, cram two fingers and a thumb in it, take about eight Fred Flintstone twinkle-toe steps, roll the ball, sit down, eat a hot dog, and drink a drink. For this you need special shoes? And when we go to get our shoes, they think we're going to steal them. They make us leave a cash deposit! Now I don't know about you, but I don't own a green and purple suit that's going to match these goofy shoes, and I definitely don't want to be seen walking around town with an 11½ on the back of my foot! And have you heard the television sportscasters cover a bowling match? It's a tough job. "So, Bob, what do you think he should do this time?"

"Well, Mary, I think he ought to knock all those pins down and let the air blow on his hand so he can do it again. What do you think?"

Unexpected Laughs

A married couple went to Utah for a ski holiday. It was a beautiful spring day with perfect snow conditions and perfect weather but long lines at the lifts. Halfway through the day the wife needed to use the restroom, but because the slopes were crowded and she wanted to make the most of the day, she kept skiing. Run after run she put it off until eventually she gave in and headed for the facilities.

Her overzealous husband pleaded, "Just one more trip up. You can go when we get to the top of the mountain." But at the top, they discovered there was no lodge. As they skied to the bottom, she was unable to hold it any longer. The woman told her husband to stand guard while she went into the trees. With her skis still on and her pants down, the woman lost her balance and came shooting out of the trees going backwards. Picking up speed, she flew across the ski run, hit the ski lift tower, and broke her leg. Her husband flagged down the ski patrol, escorted them down the mountain, and took her to the hospital.

Sitting in the emergency room trying to take her mind off the pain, she engaged another patient in conversation.

"Why are you here?" she asked.

"Lady," he responded. "You wouldn't believe what happened today. I was skiing and riding up the ski lift, when a woman came shooting out of the trees going backwards with her drawers down around her ankles. She hit the tower and broke her leg. I started laughing so hard that I fell off the ski lift and broke my arm!"

Transportation

Flight Attendants

As we were coming in for a landing at the Dallas/Fort Worth airport, our Delta Airlines jet hit heavy turbulence and bounced all over the sky. When we finally touched down, we hit loud and hard, bounced, hit again, bounced, and hit a third time, this time staying on the ground. As we taxied to the gate, the flight attendant spoke over the public address system, "Welcome to Dallas, Texas. If you enjoyed your flight, tell your friends you flew Delta. If you did not enjoy your flight, tell your friends you flew Southwest. And please remain seated with your seat belt fastened tightly while Captain Kangaroo bounces our plane to the terminal."

As we got off the plane, the elderly woman walking in front of me stopped the pilot and asked, "Did we really land, or did we get shot down?"

Idiots on the Highway

A truck driver was driving along on the freeway. A sign suddenly appeared: LOW BRIDGE. Before he could stop, he hit it and got stuck. Cars were backed up for miles.

Finally, a police car arrived. The cop got out of his car and walked around to the truck driver, put his hands on his hips, and said, "Got stuck, huh?"

The truck driver said, "No, I was delivering this bridge and ran out of gas."

Idiots in Service

Last time I had a flat tire, I pulled my truck into one of those side-of-the-road gas stations. The attendant walked out, looked at my truck, looked at me, and said, "Tahr go flat?"

I couldn't resist. I said, "Nope. I was driving around and those other three just swelled right up on me."

Engine Trouble

One day, I was on an airplane, a three-engine 727 jet. I never get nervous until I start thinking about how the plane has over thirty thousand moving parts put together by the lowest bidder. We were circling the Denver airport when the plane suddenly dipped and jolted to the left. The pilot came on the public address system, "I'm sorry, we have lost the left engine and will have to climb to gain some altitude. There will be a ten-minute delay." About nine minutes went by, and suddenly the plane jolted to the right. The pilot came back on the speaker. "We just lost the right engine and have to climb to gain some additional altitude. There will be another fifteen-minute delay."

Hearing this, the man sitting next to me leaned over and very solemnly said, "I sure hope we don't lose that last engine, or we could be up here all day!"

The Ultimate Airline Saga

I was flying from Chicago to Springfield, Illinois, on a commuter airline. It was on one of those forty-passenger prop jobs where you buy your ticket from the commuter counter, leave from a United Airlines gate, and pass by the pilot who is wearing an American Airlines hat. We took off, and the flight attendant served the usual little toy meals with plugged toy salt and pepper shakers and toy utensils. The food was an upgrade from the usual rubber chicken surprise, but I didn't eat it because the chunk of beef was so red and rare that a good veterinarian could have probably brought it back to life.

The longer we flew, the more I realized they shouldn't just have no smoking sections on airplanes, they should have no talking sections. For some reason, when certain people get their bodies into any kind of reclining position, they think it is automatic therapy and want to tell you their entire life story, beginning with DNA.

The guy next to me was hairy—I mean he had hair where most monkeys don't. And of course he was wearing a stinky tank top (for some reason hairy guys always want to show us their hair) with a vulgar slogan printed on the front of his shirt. This kills me. If I don't want to hear from this guy's mouth, why should I want to hear from his clothing?

When we landed, we came straight down. Within a hundred feet of the ground, we screeched to an abrupt halt. Since I was on the front row, I overheard the conversation between the pilot and the copilot. The pilot said, "Man, this runway's short!"

The copilot replied, "Yeah, but it's about two miles wide!"

I got off the plane and went into the terminal to retrieve my bags. Wouldn't you know it—they lost my luggage. I went by the ticket counter and overheard a man purchasing his ticket explain, "I want my luggage to go to Jamaica and I want to go to Albuquerque." The ticket lady said, "I'm sorry, but we can't do that."

The man replied, "Why? You did it last time!"

As I filled out the paperwork for my lost luggage, I overheard an elderly southern lady tearing into the man across the counter. "Don't you lie to me, don't you dare lie to me! I know that if the pilot of this plane can fly in the dark and can find Springfield, Illinois in a snowstorm, then you can find my bag!"

Another man was standing on the other side of me with his suitcase beside him on the floor. It was plastered with stickers which read Hawaii, Toronto, Oklahoma, Utah, and Florida. Seeing the suitcase, the elderly woman blurted out, "My, oh my, have you been to all those places?"

The man replied, "No, but my luggage has!"

Plane Time

Once on a college recruiting trip I was with a young player who had never flown on a plane and had no idea about time zone changes. We were going from Atlanta, Georgia, to Knoxville, Tennessee. The clerk at the counter said, "The plane leaves at 4 p.m., and you arrive fifteen minutes earlier in Knoxville at 3:45 p.m. Would you like to buy a ticket?"

The bewildered player replied, "No, I don't want a ticket. But I sure want to see the plane take off!"

The Polite Pilot

I was flying from San Francisco to Los Angeles. By the time we took off, there had been a forty-five-minute delay and everybody on board was angry. Unexpectedly, we stopped in Sacramento on the way. The flight attendant explained that there would be another forty-five-minute delay, and if we wanted to get off the aircraft, we would re-board in thirty minutes.

Everybody got off the plane except one gentleman who was blind. I had noticed him as I walked by and could tell he had flown before because his seeing-eye dog lay quietly underneath the seats in front of him throughout the entire flight. I could also tell he had flown this very flight before because the pilot approached him and, calling him by name, said, "Keith, we're here in Sacramento for almost an hour. Would you like to get off and stretch your legs?"

Keith replied, "No thanks, but maybe my dog would like to stretch his legs."

Picture this: All the people in the gate area came to a complete standstill when they looked up and saw the pilot walk off the plane with a seeing-eye dog. The pilot was even wearing sunglasses! People scattered. They not only tried to change planes, but they were also trying to change airlines!

Finding Humor

Have you seen the safety instruction card on most airlines? In the emergency exit row the card says, "If you cannot read this, please notify the flight attendant and she will change your seat assignment."

◉ ◉ ◉

What about the Delta Airlines sickness bag? To save money they have combined two signs. On one side of the bag it says: FOR MOTION DISCOMFORT. On the other side it says: OCCUPIED. Apparently you can throw up in the bag and then leave it on your seat so no one sits there while you're gone!

◉ ◉ ◉

Have you ever stayed at one of those low-budget, no-tell motels trying to save money? They want us to feel at home and welcome, and we do, until we get into our room. Suddenly, we feel violated. Everything is screwed down! You can't even pick up the remote control. You have to aim it and shoot. Even the pictures are screwed to the wall. This intrigues me. Why do they think we want to steal pictures of wheat? I prefer the hotels where the towels in your room are so fluffy you have a hard time getting your suitcase closed.

Idiots in the Neighborhood

I live in a semi-rural area. We recently had a new neighbor call the local township administrative office to request the removal of the Deer Crossing sign on our road. The reason: Many deer were being hit by cars, and he no longer wanted them to cross there.

Don't Drink and Ride

Monday night, my friend had a near-death experience that has changed him forever. We went to a bachelor party, got drunk, and went horseback riding. Everything was going fine until the horse started bouncing out of control. My friend tried with all his might to hang on but was thrown off.

Just when things could not possibly get worse, his foot got caught in the stirrup. He fell headfirst to the ground. His head continued to bounce harder and harder as the horse did not stop or even slow down.

Just as he was giving up hope and losing consciousness, the Wal-Mart manager came and unplugged it!

What's the Deal?

America—you gotta love it. What makes it the greatest country on earth? It's the land of opportunity. America is the only country in the world where an immigrant can land on shore speaking absolutely no English and be driving a taxi cab in our nation's capital on the same day!

◉ ◉ ◉

America—it's the best place to sell something because we all want a great deal. We don't want to buy tires for eighty-five dollars, so they sell them to us for $39.95. Then we need to buy all the extras: "Do you want them on your car?" (No dummy, I just want to look at them!) Twenty bucks per tire. "Do you want them balanced?" (No, I'm going to drive down the road bouncing!)

Education

Smart

When you hang around with an eighteen-year-old guy who keeps referring to the seventh grade as his senior year, it makes you feel better about yourself.

◉ ◉ ◉

Once I came home from school with a report card that had four F's and one D on it. My dad responded, "Son, looks to me like you're spending too much time on one subject!"

Rivalry

Two perfect jokes for town, state, or school rivalries. No offense intended—for illustration only:

Johnny comes home from his first day of third grade and excitedly reports, "Dad, I was the only guy in the third grade who could count from one to a hundred."

His dad says, "Good job, son. I'm proud. And remember, it's because you're from Arkansas."

Johnny comes home from his second day of school and reports, "Dad, I was the only guy in the third grade who could say his ABCs."

His dad says, "Good job, son. I'm proud. And remember, it's because you're from Arkansas."

Johnny comes home from school the third day and reports, "Dad, today we had P.E., and when we changed into our gym clothes the kids wanted to know why I was the only guy in third grade who had hair on my chest, why my feet were four times bigger than theirs, and why I was so tall. I proudly told them it was because I was from Arkansas."

His dad said, "No, no, son. It is because you are eighteen!"

⊙ ⊙ ⊙

The quarterback playing for the Aggies got hit so hard he was knocked unconscious. The coaching staff ran onto the field to help him. As the player came to, blinked his eyes, and shook his head, the assistant coach held up three fingers in front of his face and asked, "How many fingers do you count?"

The head coach immediately interrupted, "Oh man, he doesn't know that!"

Reading?

One day I was sitting on a bench on a folded newspaper. A man strolled by and asked, "Excuse me, are you reading that?" A few minutes later the same thing happened again, but this time I was ready. I was still sitting on the paper when a different man came up to me and asked if I was reading it. I stood up, turned the page, sat back down, and answered, "Yes, but I'll be done in a minute!"

Caught

A student was taking a test. Dumbfounded, he whispered to his buddy, "How close are you to the answer?"

His buddy replied, "About two seats away!"

When the test results came back the teacher accused him, "You cheated!"

He rebutted, "No, I didn't,"

"Yes, you did."

"How did you know?" he finally broke down and asked.

The teacher replied, "The girl you were sitting next to wrote on her test paper, 'Don't know the answer.' You wrote, 'me neither.'"

Lambada

Mr. Richards, our high school principal, couldn't believe his eyes. One night as he chaperoned a dance, he pulled me aside and asked, "When did they start doing this dance thing with the girl cuddled up against the guy, doing all that pelvic gyration junk?"

I smiled and answered, "It started with the movie *Dirty Dancing* and has been around for awhile. They call it the 'Lambada.'"

Mr. Richards replied, "We used to neuter dogs for doing that to our leg!"

Debatable

The other day I was at my friend's home, and his tenth-grade son came into the kitchen. With his speech impediment, he told his dad, "I-I-I w-w-wa-want t-t-t-to try out f-f-fo-for the debate team." His dad always supported him and believed in him—so he told his son he thought he could do it. The next day the son came home from school dejected. His dad asked him if he made the debate team. His son replied, "N-n-n-no. Th-th-th-they s-s-sa-said I w-w-wa-wasn't t-t-tall enough."

Pure Intelligence

Every once in a while you hear a football player express himself as a true "piece of work." "I wear a helmet (pointing to his shoulders) and shoulda-ma-pads (pointing to his head) to keep me from becoming drain bamaged. I know half this game is 90 percent mental."

◎ ◎ ◎

Sorry to say, but a lot of athletes are true "dumb jocks." As steroid poster children whose cholesterol counts are higher than their SAT scores, they easily perpetuate the "meathead" stereotype. One of my friends, Richard, a big, strong, articulate lineman, appeared on national television as a participant in the game show *Wheel of Fortune*. He was actually ahead and winning by three hundred dollars when he interrupted by asking, "Pat, may I buy a vowel, please? Can you give me a K?"

Extra Credit

Two college basketball players were flunking a class and needed some extra credit points to be eligible for that night's game. The professor explained, "If you can answer one question, you will pass and play tonight. The question is: 'Old McDonald had a ________.' I'll be back in a minute for your written responses."

The professor left, and after ten minutes of tense silence, one player grabbed his head and said to the other, "What is the answer?"

"Are you serious?" the other replied. It's easy. Old McDonald had a farm."

"Oh yeah, I remember!" He went to write it down but paused. "How do you spell farm?"

The other player couldn't believe it. "You idiot. It's easy. E-I-E-I-O!"

Pronunciation

Two men were driving through Louisiana. As they were approaching Natchidoches, they started arguing about the pronunciation of the town. They argued back and forth until they stopped for lunch.

As they stood at the counter, one asked the female employee, "Before we order, could you settle a twenty-dollar bet for us? Would you please pronounce where we are . . . very slowly?"

The lady leaned over the counter and said, "Burrrrrrgerrrrrrr Kiiiiiiiing."

He's teaching her arithmetic.
He said it was his mission.
He kissed her once, he kissed her twice
And said, "Now that's addition."

And as he added smack by smack
In silent satisfaction,
She sweetly gave the kisses back
And said, "Now that's subtraction."

Then he kissed her, she kissed him
Without an explanation.
Then both together smiled and said,
"That's multiplication."

Then Dad appeared upon the scene
And made a quick decision.
He kicked that kid three blocks away
And said, "That's long division!"

Best Lines

One Liners

Did you know that dolphins are so intelligent that within only a few weeks of captivity they can train Americans to stand at the very edge of the pool and throw them fish?

◉ ◉ ◉

Why is it that if someone tells you there are 1 billion stars in the universe, you will believe them, but if they tell you that a wall has wet paint, you will have to touch it to be sure?

◉ ◉ ◉

I've been getting into astronomy, so I installed a skylight; the people who live above me are furious.

◉ ◉ ◉

I always wanted to be the last guy on earth, just to see if all these women were lying to me.

Best Classified Ads

- 1 Man, 7 Woman Hot Tub—$850/OBO
- 2 Butchering gloves: One 5-finger glove, one 3-finger glove. Pair: $15. Call Tuesday after I get my stitches out.

- 10 Cows—Never been bred. Also, 1 gay bull for sale—Best offer.
- Nordic track $300—hardly used. Call Chubbie.
- Shakespeare's Pizza—Free chopsticks.

Best Bumper Stickers

- Forget about world peace, use your turn signal!
- You're unique—just like everybody else!

Best Signs

- There are three kinds of people: those who can count and those who can't.
- i souport publik edekasion.
- Out of my mind—back in five minutes.
- Don't even think about crossing this field unless you can run it in nine seconds. The bull does it in nine and a half!

Best Headlines

- Something Went Wrong in Jet Crash, Expert Says
- Man Steals Clock, Faces Time
- Squad Helps Dog Bite Victim
- Man Struck by Lightning, Faces Battery Charge
- Killer Sentenced to Die for Second Time in 10 Years
- Typhoon Rips Through Cemetery: Hundreds Dead
- Hospitals Sued by Seven Foot Doctors

Best Country Song Titles

- My Wife Ran off with My Best Friend and I'm Going to Miss Him Dearly

Best Pick-up Line

- May I buy you a drink so I look better?

Best Close for a Speech or Book

- I challenge you to drink, swear, steal, and lie!
- Drink from the fountain of love and friendship found in mankind.
- Swear that today will be the best day of the rest of your life.
- Steal a little extra time to do something special for someone when you know you won't get the credit.
- When you lie down at night, thank the God above that you live in the greatest country in the world!

Best Signs

- In a veterinarian's waiting room: "Be back in 5 minutes. Sit! Stay!"
- On maternity room door: "Push, Push, Push."
- Outside a muffler shop: "No appointment necessary; we'll hear you coming."
- In the front yard of a funeral home: "Drive carefully, we'll wait."
- Door of a plastic surgeon's office: "We can help pick your nose."
- At a tire shop in Milwaukee: "Invite us to your next blowout."
- Sign at the psychic's employment hotline: "Don't call us, we'll call you."

- At an optometrist's office: "If you don't see what you're looking for, you've come to the right place."
- On an electrician's truck: "Let us remove your shorts."
- In a counselor's office: "Growing old is mandatory, growing wise is optional."

Best Quotes

"We're going to turn this team around 360 degrees."—Jason Kidd, upon being drafted to the NBA.

⊙ ⊙ ⊙

"I've never had major knee surgery on any other part of my body." —Winston Bennett, University of Kentucky basketball forward.

⊙ ⊙ ⊙

I don't make political jokes. Too many of them get elected.

⊙ ⊙ ⊙

Bill Clinton is getting twelve million dollars for his memoirs, and Hillary got eight million dollars for hers. That's twenty million dollars for two people who, for eight years, repeatedly testified that they couldn't remember anything!

⊙ ⊙ ⊙

In an interview, former Vice President Dan Quail asked Mikail Gorbechov, "What's that red thing on your forehead?"

Gorby answered, "It's a birthmark."

Quail asked, "How long have you had that?"

⊙ ⊙ ⊙

Former Vice President Al Gore screwed up twice in the same week when he said, "It is wonderful to be here in the great state of Chicago." Gore then said, "I was recently on a tour of Latin America, and the only regret I have was that I didn't study Latin harder in school so I could talk to those people."

⊙ ⊙ ⊙

"If you're not a liberal at age twenty, you have no heart. If you're not a conservative at age forty, you have no brain."—Winston Churchill

⊙ ⊙ ⊙

"That lowdown scoundrel deserves to be kicked to death by a jackass, and I'm just the one to do it."—Congressional Candidate in Texas.

⊙ ⊙ ⊙

"Researchers have discovered that chocolate produces some of the same reactions in the brain as marijuana. The researchers also discovered other similarities between the two, but they can't remember what they are."—Matt Lauer on NBC's Today Show.

Best Answering Machine Messages

A is for academics, B is for beer. One of those reasons is why I'm not here.

⊙ ⊙ ⊙

Hi, this is Dan.
If you are the phone company, I already sent the money.
If you are my parents, please send money.
If you are my financial institution, you didn't lend me enough money.
If you are my friend, you owe me money.
If you are female, don't worry, I have plenty of money.
If you are a solicitor, I don't need lightbulbs, my carpets cleaned, or my picture taken.
I gave to charity at the office and I am happy with my phone service.
If you're still with me, I am probably home.
I'm just avoiding someone I don't like.
Leave me a message, and if I don't call back, it's you!

⊙ ⊙ ⊙

You've reached the car phone of _______. I'm sorry I'm IN right now. If you'll please leave a message I will call you when I'm OUT again."

You shouldn't try to teach a pig to sing. It's a waste of your time and it annoys the pig!

—*Mark Twain*

Do not let what you cannot do interfere with what you can do!

On the Job

Business

A businessman was driving in the country when he came upon a sheepherder on the side of the road.

He stopped and asked, "If I can tell you how many sheep you have, can I have one?"

The sheepherder agreed, so the man pulled out his laptop, did some calculations, and proclaimed, "You have 1,455 sheep." The sheepherder agreed and the man went into the field, picked his animal, and put it in the back of his car.

Before he drove away, the sheepherder asked, "If I can tell you what you do for a living, can I have my animal back?" The man agreed.

"You are a consultant," the sheepherder said.

"Yes, I am. How could you tell?"

The sheepherder replied, "You told me something that I already know. Now, can I have my dog back?"

Quick Thinking

A man was given a promotion in his company. The president called him in and said, "We are impressed with your leadership skills. We need you to move to Detroit."

The man soured, "I don't want to move to Detroit. The only things Detroit has are good hockey teams and ugly women."

The president was offended, "What do you mean? My wife is from Detroit."

The man quickly replied, "Oh yeah, which team does she play for?"

Idiots at Work

I was signing the receipt for my credit card purchase when the clerk noticed that I had never signed my name on the back of the credit card. She informed me that she could not complete the transaction unless the card was signed. When I asked why, she explained that it was necessary to compare the signature on the credit card with the signature I just signed on the receipt. So I signed the credit card in front of her. She carefully compared that signature to the one I signed on the receipt. As luck would have it, they matched!

Who Is This?

A young soldier was working in the army supply building when he answered a telephone call.

"Inventory check," the deep voice demanded.

The soldier reported, "We have twenty-five tanks, 2,500 rifles, and one fat-headed sergeant's Jeep."

The voice on the other end said, "What?"

The soldier repeated, "We have twenty-five tanks, 2,500 rifles, and one fat-headed sergeant's Jeep."

Angrily, the voice asked, "Do you know who this is?"

The soldier replied, "No."

"This is the Sergeant!" he screamed.

The soldier gasped and asked, "Do you know who this is?"

The Sergeant answered, "No."

The soldier sighed, "Good. Bye, bye, fat-head!"

Slap!

A young Marine and his commanding officer board a train headed through the mountains of Switzerland. They can find no place to sit except for two seats right across the aisle from a young woman and her grandmother.

After a while, it is obvious that the young woman and the young soldier are interested in each other because they are giving each other "looks."

Soon the train passes into a tunnel and it is pitch black. There is a sound of the smack of a kiss followed by the sound of the smack of a slap. When the train emerges from the tunnel, the four sit there without saying a word.

The grandmother is thinking to herself: "It was very brash for that young soldier to kiss my granddaughter, but I'm glad she slapped him."

The commanding officer is sitting there thinking, "I didn't know the young Marine was brave enough to kiss the girl, but I sure wish she hadn't missed him when she slapped and hit me!"

The young woman was sitting and thinking: "I'm glad the soldier kissed me, but I wish my grandmother had not slapped him!"

The young Marine sat there with a satisfied smile on his face. He thought to himself. "Life is good. When does a fellow have the chance to kiss a beautiful girl and slap his commanding officer all at the same time!"

You Know You Work in the 90s If . . .

1. You've sat at the same desk for four years and worked for three different companies.

2. Your company welcome sign is attached with Velcro.

3. Your resume is on a diskette in your pocket.

4. Your To Do list includes "go home."

What the Doctor Said

A man was having chest pains, and his wife insisted on taking him to the doctor. The doctor examined him and sent him out of the office, telling him to send his wife in for a private consultation.

The doctor told the man's wife that if she didn't wake up early every morning, deliver his breakfast in bed, rub his back, and drive him to work, he would die.

The doctor continued, "You must then fix and deliver a fresh, hot lunch to him every day at work, and rub his feet and back again, or he will die."

The doctor then concluded, "And when you pick him up from work and drive him home, you need to have a wonderful dinner ready for him, rub his back again, and cater to his every need until you tuck him into bed. If you don't do these things, he will die."

They left the doctor's office and started driving home.

Her husband asked, "You were in there a long time. What did the doctor say?"

His wife looked at him and solemnly answered, "You are going to die."

Temperature

A bossy businessman learned things the hard way after ordering his nurses around as if they were his employees. But the head nurse stood up to him.

One morning she entered his room and announced, "I have to take your temperature." After complaining for several minutes, he finally settled down, crossed his arms, and opened his mouth.

"No, I'm sorry," the nurse stated. "I can't use an oral thermometer." This started another round of complaining, but eventually he rolled over and bared his bottom.

After feeling the nurse insert the thermometer, he heard her announce, "I have to get something. Now you stay just like that until I get back!" She left the door to his room open and he cursed under his breath as he heard people walking past his door laughing.

After almost an hour, the man's doctor came into the room.

"What's going on here?" asked the doctor.

Angrily, the man answered, "What's the matter, Doc? Haven't you ever seen someone having their temperature taken?"

"Yes," said the doctor. "But never with a carnation!"

What's the Matter?

A man walks into a doctor's office. He has a cucumber up his nose, a carrot in his left ear, and a banana in his right ear. "Doctor, what's the matter with me?"

"You're not eating properly."

Defenseless

A defense attorney was cross-examining a police officer during a felony trial:

"Officer, did you see my client fleeing the scene?"

"No, sir, but a fellow officer provided the description of the offender running several blocks away."

"A fellow officer gave you the information? Do you trust your fellow officers?"

"Yes, sir, with my life."

"With your life?"

"Yes, sir."

"If you trust your fellow officers with your life, then why do you find it necessary to lock your locker in a room you share with those officers?"

"You see, sir, we share the building with a court complex, and sometimes defense attorneys have been known to walk through that room."

With that, the courtroom erupted in laughter, and a prompt recess was called.

Lawyering

A lawyer defending a man accused of burglary tried this creative defense:

"My client merely inserted his arm into the window and removed a few trifling articles. His arm is not himself, and I fail to see how you can punish the whole individual for an offense committed by his limb."

"Well put," the judge replied. "Using your logic, I sentence the defendant's arm to one year's imprisonment. He can accompany it or not, as he chooses."

The defendant smiled. With his lawyer's assistance he detached his artificial limb, laid it on the bench, and walked out.

Career Opportunities

You see a gorgeous girl at a party. You go up to her and say, "I'm a fantastic lover." That's Direct Marketing.

You're at a party with a bunch of friends and see a gorgeous girl. One of your friends goes up to her and, pointing at you, says, "He's a fantastic lover." That's Advertising.

You see a gorgeous girl at a party. You go up to her and get her telephone number. The next day you call and say, "Hi, I'm a fantastic lover." That's Telemarketing.

You're at a party and see a gorgeous girl. You get up and straighten your tie, walk up to her, and pour her a drink. You open the door for her, pick up her bag after she drops it, offer her a ride, and then say, "By the way, I'm a fantastic lover." That's Public Relations.

You're at a party and see a gorgeous girl. She walks up to you and says, "I hear you're a fantastic lover." That's Brand Recognition.

Any Questions?

A man entered a New York attorney's office and asked what his rates were. "It's seventy-five dollars for three questions," the attorney replied.

"Isn't that awfully high?" the man asked.

"Perhaps," the lawyer stated. "And what is your final question?"

The Jerk

A guy walks into a bar and shouts, "Motivational speakers are jerks!"

A man stands up and replies, "I take offense to that remark."

"Why, are you a motivational speaker?"

"No, I'm a jerk!"

PhD

All of the information in the world does not make a person successful. It's like the guy who has three PhDs: one in philosophy, one in psychology, and one in sociology. He doesn't have a job, but at least he can explain why!

Work

For a couple years I've been blaming it on lack of sleep and too much pressure from my job, but now I found out the real reason: I'm tired because I'm overworked.

The population of this country is 237 million, of which 104 million are retired.

That leaves 133 million to do the work.

There are 85 million in school, which leaves 48 million to do the work.

Of this there are 29 million employed by the federal government, plus 2.8 million in the Armed Forces, which leaves 16.2 million to do the work.

Take from the total the 14.8 million people who work for state governments and that leaves 1.4 million to do the work.

At any given time there are 188,000 people in hospitals, leaving 1,212,000 to do the work.

Now, there are 1,211,988 people in prisons.

That leaves just two people to do the work.

You and me.

And you're sitting here reading this joke book?

0 26575 70381 8